love letter to anyone

DESTROYED OR DECEIVED BY RELIGION

DENISE WOODARD SMITH

ISBN: 979-8-9922596-0-5 eBook
ISBN: 979-8-9922596-1-2 Print
ISBN: 979-8-9922596-2-9 Audio Book

First paperback edition September 2025
Book design by Damonza

This is a non-fiction book for informational purposes only.
The author shares each event truthfully, exactly as they happened.

As Mom and YaYa, I'm leaving my life story to my children and my grandchildren so they can better understand me through the stories that have impacted my life and that explain why my faith was and is so important to me.

PART ONE

First of all, I'm excited to finally be writing these words of encouragement to you, presented as if they were a direct letter from our Heavenly Father to you, His beloved children. He loves each and every one of you so much. I have felt guilty that it has taken me so long to get this letter written, but I feel finally that today is the day, a special day, to keep my promise, as it is Father's Day.

You see, this letter became necessary because several years ago, while I was sleeping, I heard a loud, distinctive voice call out my name: "Denise!" I was asleep at the time, but I awoke startled, blinking my eyes awake, and then I heard it again: "Denise!" I looked around, and then up, and I saw the face of Jesus clearly! Only His face, the same face we all see in the pictures of Him. A man with long, dark, flowing hair. He said in a loud, bold voice, "I am coming very, very soon!" It scared me. He said it with an urgency I'll never forget. I closed my eyes, and then I quickly covered my head. It was startling.

I've never had anything like that happen before. It almost makes me ashamed that I reacted that way to someone I trust and love so much. After those brief moments and events I have just described, the experience was over, and I remember thinking, *You came to see me, and that's all You had to say? Couldn't You have revealed something extra?*

After I thought about it, I realized that what He said was the most important message Jesus could have reminded me of. His voice had such an urgency that I'll never ever forget it. I don't think more powerful words could have been spoken. "I am coming very, very soon!" It felt like a father desperately crying out to his children, "Hurry! Get ready, I'm coming for you!" It was as if He were standing over the water and one of His children were drowning. It sounded like He was urgently pleading for help to save His child from dying. Just like any of us would feel if we witnessed one of our children in distress. He wants help to save each and every one of His children before He returns and it's too late to offer this help.

I have tried to share this vision with whomever I could, feeling a responsibility that He was trusting me to do so. Then the feeling grew stronger that I should share my experiences in a book so that as many people as possible could hear and feel His heart. The simple message He wants you all to know before it's too late. Life has led me to be busy, distracted, and exhausted. Yet the gnawing has been in my heart, urging me to release His message to you. It is a simple and direct message, one of love, peace, and joy, not of guilt.

I can totally understand why people would be turned off by religion. Several so-called churches and religions out there have caused so much destruction in people's lives. They have forced them to secrecy in following their complicated rules. They have taken a lot of their money and kept people from family members who may not follow their rules or beliefs. They've guilted people into doing things they know are not right, causing a great deal of mistrust in God. People have been abused by leaders in the Church—leaders who should've protected their church members.

The world is also watching how Christians are behaving, and I think they are seeing a group of people who are not showing what they are supposed to represent—acceptance of all of God's children. There is too much judgment of others. We are forgetting what it means to be a follower of God, and we are turning a lot of people off, discouraging them from giving God a chance in their lives. Enough is enough! Let's get it together!

This letter is meant for anyone devastated by religion. I want you to heal. Be made whole and start your life afresh. Let go of the past, be set free, and start anew! It is never too late. I can't imagine going through this life without leaning on Jesus and holding His hand through each and every day. Especially during these tough times of uncertainty. Whether it's the fear of the recurring pandemics around the world, losing a job or a family member, or having no one to trust and look up to for strength and peace. Remember, don't put your eyes on man; they will fail and disappoint you. Rather look up and keep your eyes on Jesus. He's the one to put your faith in, not man.

After you finish reading this letter, that is what I pray you find: healing, peace, and joy. Through Jesus, I'm going to explain in a simple way how you can experience these blessings. It doesn't mean it will be easy. This isn't Heaven. We have free will. Unlike religion, God gives us choices. We will have consequences to our actions, but God will never leave us. He will be there every step of the way.

PART TWO

God sent His son Jesus to redeem us. He had to die on the cross and then arise to give us a second chance, a promise of eternal life with Him. Jesus was a simple man, a carpenter. He didn't have a complicated degree, and He didn't act like He was better than or superior to anyone else. He lived and walked His faith by showing love and kindness and not judging others. He didn't force anyone to follow Him, but through His gentle, loving Spirit, people wanted to.

A strong example that stands out in the Bible, in my opinion, is the Parable of the Good Samaritan (Luke 10:25–37). That's the one where a man is injured and lying on the side of the road in need of help. Then a priest walks by but doesn't stop to help because it's the Sabbath—a day of rest and worship at the temple. He did not want to be distracted because he needed to quickly get on his way. Then a Levite came along, and he, too, walked on the other side of the road, offering no help. Eventually a Samaritan passed that way, and he helped the man.

This is an example of how people get caught in the complicated trap of the rules of religion and their busy lives, totally forgetting how the simple act of showing mercy and helping someone in need should come first. It is so simple. Jesus just wants us to accept Him, love Him and love others, show mercy and kindness, and do the right thing. Treat others as you'd want to be treated. Simply be His eyes, hands, and feet. It's that simple. He just wants a relationship with you.

Another example I love in the Bible is about the woman who was caught in adultery (John 8:3–11). In this story, religious leaders bring a woman before Jesus, accusing her of adultery and stating that the law of Moses calls for stoning. Jesus, however, responds with compassion, saying, "Let any one of you who is without sin throw the first stone at her." Meaning we all have sinned; none of us are perfect, but He still loves all of us. So, as Christians, let's remember not to judge anyone but show love to all of God's children because none of us are perfect. We are all guilty of sinning.

PART THREE

I want to share why I know there is more to this life than what we see around us. This faith in God and the belief that He sent His son to die on the cross and that He arose from death so we can have a second chance at eternity with Him are real. Heaven is real. It's not just a fantasy. Don't give up hope. You have a second chance to believe in God. To love Him and reach Heaven. Hang in there. He will forgive anything in your past provided you are remorseful and seek forgiveness. As soon as you ask Him to forgive you, acknowledging that you have sinned, it is wiped away and forgotten. You must forget the wrongs and the hurts of the past and forgive others so you can move forward fresh and new. It is never too late!

The weight of the past hurts will be gone. It will be so worth forgiving everything that happened in the past, as it sets you free to move forward with your new life, believing and trusting God every step of the way. Ask Him to take you by the right hand and ask Him to help you take each step with Him. You are never alone. In your mind you can say, "God, I am bone of your bone, blood of your blood, flesh of your flesh." There is power in these words!

Again, I want to share a few experiences that happened to me throughout my life that proved to me Jesus is real—not just a myth. Heaven is real, but so is Hell.

For thirty-five years of my life, I have worked in a job that involved caring for elderly people. I have seen a lot of life and death. I want to share meaningful events to help encourage you to believe God is real and show you why it's important to believe and give God a second (or first) chance at winning back your heart. I guarantee you'll never regret it.

The beauty of walking with God is that it's simple and not meant to be complicated. You don't have to pay money to get a degree to be part of the religion. You just have to pray and to acknowledge Him and accept Him in your heart and ask Him to forgive your sins. And really mean it. Let Him know you believe He is the one and only God who sent His son to show us how to live. Jesus died on the cross and then arose to give us eternal life. You can read God's words in the Holy Bible (the New International Version, the NIV, is the easiest to understand). It's good to start the New Testament with the Book of Matthew. This is the perfect book to start with because it is the Gospel about Jesus's life, and it will help you understand Him better. After this, read the Gospels of Mark, Luke, and John. Then simply try and be His hands, eyes, and feet.

Take one day at a time and try to be more like Him. What would He do? How would He act? And so on. It's simple. Talk to Him daily and build a relationship with Him. Thank Him daily for all the little blessings He is putting in your path. Pray for His will in the decisions you make. God knows what's best for us, and He loves us more than anything. You should have a sense of peace and walk in confidence as you become the new you! No more fear or confusion—you never walk alone. He is always with you, a constant comfort and companion. Man fails us, but He doesn't. Don't look to or depend on man. Instead, look up to God to guide and protect you in all of your decisions.

Here are some of my experiences to encourage you and increase your faith that God is real. I've learned He cares about each individual and knows what the desires of your heart are, no matter how small they might be. Also, another lesson I've learned is that He won't give you more than you can handle at any one time. It doesn't mean we won't get close to our limit, but He will faithfully do something or put someone in our path to help us, so nothing is too much to handle at the time. I've gotten close to my limit many times, but then I'll remind God, "I'm not Hercules. Lord, your shoulders are bigger than mine; take this and help me!"

As I have mentioned, I took care of elderly people for thirty-five years. It was a business our family was involved in for many years. I got into it unexpectedly. We cared for the elderly out of our home. We raised our children in our home while we cared for these residents. It was a rewarding job, but a very difficult one, as it involved working seven days a week, twenty-four hours a day. Prior to this, after I was first married, my husband enlisted in the US Army, and we were sent to Germany for the last year of his four-year commitment.

In high school, after having taken a French class, I always dreamed of going to Europe. My teacher instilled in me a love of the language, food, and countryside. I longed to go there one day. My husband went first, to Germany, and found us a place to live. I remember that as I was grabbing my suitcases and my two-year-old daughter, I heard on the TV, on *Good Morning America*, the news anchor saying, "If you go to Germany today, the dollar–mark exchange rate is at an all-time high."

I thought, *What a coincidence! I'm going there today!* I didn't realize what the exchange rate meant. My husband was an E2, a private first class (PFC), and we made very little money. But he found a fully furnished farmhouse for $100 (given the exchange rate at the time), and that is why it was so important for the dollar–mark exchange rate to be high—we could get a great many marks for our American dollars. The conversion rate made our few dollars stretch far! It felt like we were living like royalty compared to what we could afford in the States. We had money to travel, eat out, and sample all the wonderful foods in the region. It was an amazing time.

God helped him to find us the perfect house in a small village with wonderful landlords who let us use their garden. They even put up a swing and built a sandbox for our daughter. We had talked to friends, who said, "If you can find a house in a small village, you will be able to immerse yourself in the culture. You can live in a big city or visit one anytime if you want to." It was so true.

I learned how to cook German dishes from my neighbors. Our house and yard were where all the neighborhood children would gather. I would make cookies for them, and they would try to teach me how to read German. I met only a couple of people who spoke English. It was fun to see our two-year-old daughter play with the German children. They were having fun, but they couldn't understand each other's language. I often heard the children repeat what sounded to me like "kokomo." I later found out it was "*herkommen*" and meant "come here." However, somehow the children found a way to understand one another. The language barrier didn't stop them from having a good time together. We can learn from children. Learn to be tolerant and accept each other even though we are different.

Another memory that stood out while I was over there was the first day I arrived in Germany, when my husband took me to the army base to look around. He showed me the activity center, where they were having a raffle to win a paid trip for two to Paris! It sounded so amazing! After we looked at the rest of the base, we went back to hear who'd won the trip. I couldn't believe my ears. They called out, "Denise Smith!" I had won! I couldn't believe it. God knew the desire of my heart was to travel and to go to Paris. What a beginning! I didn't have to work, and we'd be in Germany for only a year. But in that time we traveled to many places, seeing some of the most amazing, beautiful countryside and history you can imagine. Everything was so cheap. We didn't have credit cards and paid for everything in cash. It was like a year's vacation.

Several other experiences that stood out during that time included church bells that would ring daily. I enjoyed hearing their soothing sound first thing in the morning. But later in the day the sound of their chime changed and took on a different meaning. There would be a warning signal that rang out, as it had done continually since WWII. It had such an eerie, haunting sound to it as it echoed through the village. That left a lasting impression on me, being from America and never having heard anything like that in my life. I just pictured what it was like in those streets and in those homes during the war. Most all the houses in the German village were at least two hundred years old. It heightened my sense of appreciation for little things, such as being safe and free and having food and water when I needed or wanted it. I learned to not take things for granted.

PART FOUR

While in Germany, I had two major events happen to me that will be forever etched into my brain and that I will never forget.

The first incident occurred shortly after arriving in Germany. My husband, who was a nuclear weapons specialist, had a position that meant we, as a family, had restricted areas of travel. One day, his specialty training had him away from home on a military mission. So, my two-year-old daughter and I were left home alone for several days. The front of the two-hundred-year-old house in which we lived in the small village was on the edge of the road, separated only by a narrow sidewalk. We were the only Americans in the village except for an elderly gentleman whom we had only just met. He was an ex-serviceman who had married a German woman, and they lived up the hill.

One evening, my little daughter lay beside me asleep on the bed when I heard what sounded like voices outside my bedroom window. I peered through the curtain and could not believe my eyes! Outside my window stood several men in military uniforms, armed with machine guns, and they were speaking a language I couldn't recognize or understand. I didn't recognize their uniforms either. I was paralyzed with fear. I thought for sure they were coming to take us hostage because of my husband's security clearance and special nuclear weapons knowledge. This was a time of terrorism, the mid-1980s, with Gaddafi in power in Libya. I was petrified they could see me and hear me breathing. I looked over to the bed and thanked God my little girl was safe and sound asleep and unaware of my fear. Still paralyzed by fear and afraid to make a sound, I immediately prayed to God Almighty for protection. This was just a little too close for comfort.

I felt so alone in this foreign country that night. I didn't even know how to dial for emergency or police help. These little things we take for granted in the comfort of our home country. As I was praying, afraid to breathe or move, I remembered I had recently met the only person in the village who spoke English—the American just up the hill. I would never otherwise have remembered his phone number, except it was an easy one (555), and he had only just given it to me in case I ever needed anything. Praise God. How much easier could God have made it for me: recently meeting someone who spoke English with a phone number so easy to recall! (If I have learned anything, it is that He will put someone in your path when He knows you'll need them the most).

Gratefully, God cleared my mind long enough to remember my neighbor's phone number. I carefully crawled on my stomach across the bedroom floor. Thankfully, the bedroom door was open and led directly into the front living room. I carefully reached for the phone. Out of breath, it hurt to whisper to this elderly man in the middle of the night, telling him to hurry to my home because terrorists were coming to get me. It's a wonder I didn't give him a heart attack. A short while later, I heard a knock at the door. I heard the familiar language of English. The elderly man said everything was okay. The armed men were just French soldiers out on maneuvers, conducting a military exercise with local forces.

He laughed and said, "You should invite them in for burgers."

I replied, "I'm sorry, but I'm in no mood for entertaining!"

Looking back, I wish I had done so because that would be a memory I'd never forget. I want to add that I didn't recognize the French spoken because of my intense fear. I was so anxious, especially with my young daughter in the house, that it was hard to discern what I was hearing. Besides, I only took a basic course in French, and different parts of the country speak different dialects.

Again, this was a heightened time of terrorism with Gaddafi in power in Libya. I didn't realize he had threatened to blow up Frankfurt Airport the day we went to pick up my sister there. We saw German soldiers with machine guns everywhere at the airport and its surroundings. The Germans don't mess around when they increase their security!

The second major incident that happened while I was in Germany was while my sister was still visiting with us.

My sister, my two-year-old daughter, Sarah, and I went on a bus tour to Spain for a week. This was in the mid-eighties when nobody had cell phones. My husband knew the approximate time of day we were due back. But we had some delays, causing us to arrive two hours late. It was a small, remote military base that we were returning to, and when we arrived, my husband wasn't there waiting for us. I looked around and noticed our car parked up on a small hill. I walked up to it and couldn't believe my eyes! The driver's side was completely smashed into the center of the car. If you looked at it, you would know instantly that the driver, presumably my husband, must've been killed by the impact. I realized that the military had no way to communicate and let me know what had happened. We were gone for a week, and no one but my husband knew where we went. It was the sickest sight I've ever encountered unexpectedly. The car looked perfect from a different angle except that the driver's seat and door were completely gone! It was a BMW, which was a well-made vehicle. I knew he must have died in the accident because we always and faithfully wore our seat-belts, and the seat was gone. With the autobahn having no maximum speed limit, they drove at high speeds in Germany. You can imagine what a horrifying scene that was to walk up on.

I can only tell you how I pleaded for the peace I talk about that God gives to people in difficult times. I couldn't understand how, but almost at once I was filled with a peace that defied explanation. It didn't make sense. I was also in a state of shock, but I remember experiencing a calming peace from head to toe. Again, I'm so thankful for those times of peace when you need it the most.

Then, thank God, all of a sudden my husband walked up to me. Not hurt and all in one piece! He said he had been waiting for us, but he had to quickly leave to go to the bathroom! He said he didn't know why, but he just didn't wear his seatbelt when he drove that day. He didn't think about it; it just happened that he forgot to fasten the seatbelt. He had never done that before. All I can say is that if he'd worn it, he would've been pinned in the seat and killed with that impact. God protects us and works mysteriously behind the scenes. Thankfully, it wasn't my husband's time to go. It was so amazing that he wasn't injured at all!

Looking back, we were not fully aware of all the terrorism going on around us. Because, although we had a TV, we never watched it. It was all in German. I'm glad I didn't know how bad things were because I would've been too afraid to walk out my front door. Instead, I enjoyed one of the best years of my life traveling all over Europe. This is just a reminder to me of how God won't give you more than you can handle. In my worst time of fear, I remembered I met a man in my village who spoke English, and his number was so simple that I remembered it! Trust me, God is so faithful that way. He had my husband forget to put on his seatbelt when normally it was something he automatically did, and on a day when this simple omission would save his life! Do you see how wonderfully He takes care of all the details? I've also learned that if it's not your time, you'll survive, but if it is, you won't.

PART FIVE

I got to experience this trip of a lifetime at a time when the dollar–mark exchange rate was the highest in many years, but it dropped quickly just as we left. I remember reading that Americans who arrived in Germany just after we left couldn't afford to travel and enjoy the foods and experiences I'd enjoyed because the dollar dropped so low that everything was too expensive. That would've broken my heart.

Little did I know that after that year of not working and constantly traveling, I would be making an unexpected change. I would be getting into a family business of caring for the elderly, a difficult twenty-four-seven job, for many years! Those memories of all the wonderful traveling I did carried me through some tough times.

Here is an example of one of the toughest times I've had to endure in my marriage. A couple of years after we started our care home, my husband, who was also working as a restaurant manager at the time, came home and said he wanted to leave me. He was working with a waitress who he enjoyed spending time with after work. It was a complete shock to me. I was totally blindsided. I had no idea. I can honestly say I never cheated on him during our entire relationship. He was my first love and my first boyfriend after high school. So, he is the one and only guy I have ever been with. I didn't realize how innocent and very naïve I was at the time, even at my age. I grew up very sheltered in a Christian home.

So, he just left that day, free as a bird. No responsibilities. I was left with a sweet daughter ready to start kindergarten. I had the care home with the elderly people I was caring for and all the bills to go with it. I wouldn't have made it without God's strength to help me get through. My situation was devastating and overwhelming. I was left to hold everything together.

About a month after he left, I started feeling so tired, sick, and nauseous. I didn't know if it was the stress of what was happening in my life or something else that was the cause. I couldn't believe it when I found out I was pregnant! I couldn't believe the timing. Really? But I was also so happy because I'd wanted another child and a little playmate for my daughter. To this day I tease my eldest daughter, Sarah, and say, "Remember the blue dot? That was your sister!" The blue dot was on my pregnancy test! That moment was a true highlight during that difficult time.

Getting back to my husband … I was so hurt, confused, and disappointed with my husband that I didn't want to tell him about my pregnancy. I didn't want him to come back to me and our daughter just because of the baby. But my doctor said it was important to let him know. He ended up being gone an entire year, and then we ended up getting back together. It was a very lonely and difficult time in my life. Only because of God covering me in peace could I get through that time of abandonment without becoming as bitter or angry as I might have.

This experience left a very special spot in my heart for single parents. My heart breaks for them. They have a very heavy load to carry. They have to do the work of both mother and father. They have to be responsible for the entire household. It's an exhausting job. It's very lonely not to be able to share highlights of your day or your kid's day with your partner. Also, if the ex-spouse is not in a healthy space, there can be a lot of mental games involved in the parenting of the children. So, it's a loss for everyone involved.

Many times it's the father who looks like the fun guy, because when he has the kids, he takes them out to make up for his lack of time with them. Whereas the mom is exhausted and on a tight budget, without any extra money to spend on fun. She is lucky to survive and keep the household functioning. The sad part is that, statistically, single-parent families make up the majority of the families out there. My heart aches for them. I don't mean to say just moms are suffering, because it's hard on the fathers too. And some fathers have the children for the majority of the time. It's just devastating for everyone involved. The heartbreak kids feel can last a lifetime. But God can help heal those wounds.

So, if you know any single-parent families, please pray for them and think about any act of kindness you could do for them. Offer to watch the kids so the single parent can have some quiet time to themselves. Offer to get them some groceries or drop off dinner so they don't have to cook. Anything would be so appreciated. I would love to hear of any kind act you do to help others in need. That's an example of being God's hands, eyes, and feet. You might even ask the local school if they know of any single families that you could offer to help in some way.

PART SIX

I'd like to share several miracles that have happened in my family, simply to encourage you and remind you God is real and that it's worth finding Him and having a relationship with Him. Nothing complicated, no rules like the chains that religion can put on you. I'm not against organized religion as such. I've just seen and heard how several religions out there have destroyed lives. They've made people feel guilty, believing they'll never be worthy of God's or Jesus's love. Religion can make it so complicated to follow their rules that you forget what you are even following. It was meant to be so simple that anyone could understand it. Just have a relationship with Jesus. Talk to Him. Thank Him for giving you a second chance at eternal life again. Ask Him to flood you with His peace. In the most difficult times, He can cover you with peace. It won't make sense how and why you feel a sense of peace at a difficult time; just accept it. As this world becomes crazy, confusing, and fearful, you can stay calm and know God is in control. Don't worry about things. Hand all your concerns to Him—He can handle it!

Here are a couple of examples of how God protected my family through the years.

One morning, my daughter Sarah was heading off to school, driving herself. Just down the street was a busy intersection. She was stopped at the intersection when a truck blew through the red light and hit my daughter's car, pushing it into the traffic. A woman who was trying to cross the street at the time was struck and flew up on my daughter's windshield. Sarah wasn't hurt, and she got out of the car to try to help the woman who had been hit. I thought that was very brave of her, considering she was only in high school. No surprise, she's been an amazing nurse since then. Months later, my daughter would point out the woman, who regularly walked down the street from our house. I would smile and pray for her every time I saw her, thanking God for protecting my daughter and this woman during the accident. I noticed the woman walked with a limp.

Then I discovered my husband had kept a secret from me for an entire year. That woman had hurt her leg and hip and needed surgery, and she was suing our auto insurance because the guy who blew through the red light and caused the accident was nowhere to be found. My husband was hoping and praying she would accept our insurance offer of $100,000, as that was all our insurance would cover. Our insurance said claims like this happen all the time and that people can and do lose their homes and everything they own. My husband was so afraid she would want more money and that we'd lose our home and business and possibly everything else. I never realized how close we came to being homeless.

I'm thankful God put it in my heart to pray for that

woman every time I saw her. Little did I know I was praying for someone whose heart, I think, God was trying to change to protect us. Well, it took a year before the insurance called to let us know she decided to settle for the $100,000! Thank God we were covered! I was upset with my husband for not telling me. I told him I could've been praying about it for all that time, but I guess I already was and didn't know it! My husband didn't want me to stress about it, as he knew it would take a long time to settle. God sure does have mysterious ways of working on our behalf.

My younger daughter, Ashley, had a terrible car accident at that same horribly dangerous intersection. She was trying to make a left turn, and someone blew through the red light. My daughter's car spun in circles in the middle of the busy intersection, and God shielded her and protected her! Miraculously, nobody else hit her as she was spinning uncontrollably. I can't imagine how vulnerable and helpless she felt. I'm so thankful she knew God was right there with her. She was stunned, in shock, and sore, but praise God, she walked away! God is so good and faithful.

My son's family was in a horrific accident too. He was driving with his wife and son when the blinding sun hit at just the wrong angle on his windshield, and he literally couldn't see a thing. As he was going through an intersection, he hit another car head-on, and as he spun around, another car coming from the other direction hit him with a side-on impact.

It's an absolute miracle that they all walked away relatively unharmed and that nobody involved was killed. I'm so thankful for how God protected them and still amazed that they were only sore with bruises. It was an unbelievable scene. How quickly they could all have been killed. I'm also thankful their precious little dog was not in the car.

Again, if it's not your time, you can survive some incredible circumstances.

PART SEVEN

Here are a few examples of God being there for me and my family when no one else was. One example involves my brother, who has had several medical issues. Once, late on the night before he was scheduled for surgery, a male nurse came into his room and told him he should not have the surgery. He said that if he had the scheduled surgery, he would not survive it because the doctors had not yet discovered that he had a serious blood issue. Later, nobody knew who that nurse was. I strongly feel it was an angel appearing in human form to be a shield of protection for my brother.

Another time, many years later, my brother, who has severe scoliosis and a metal rod in his spine, had a similar experience. His doctor discovered that my brother had a loose screw in his spine that was rubbing against his spinal cord, causing severe pain. The doctor said he also saw infection in the bone. Surgery would be extremely risky, and no doctor was willing to take on that risk. So, my brother and my mom went to the Mayo Clinic. It was their last hope. They sat there while the last possible doctor they could consult told them that he was sorry, but there was too much risk, and he wouldn't be able to do the surgery.

My brother said that at that moment he looked out of the window and thought, *This is it*. But my mom looked at my brother and said, "You've got God, David."

The doctor left the room and then, after a while, came back in and said he'd do the surgery! The surgery was a success, and there was no infection in the bone! The same doctor has been a lifesaver and has performed other surgeries on my brother since, and all have been successful.

Another experience my brother had was years ago when he and my mom went to the corner shopping center to pick up an air filter. My mom waited in the car, and my brother ran into the store and asked where the air filters were. He was told, "In aisle eleven." He went down the aisle and couldn't find any. He looked along the other aisle. Then he went back and asked someone else, and they also said, "Aisle eleven." So he went back and double-checked—nothing! He looked at a couple of surrounding aisles. Nothing.

At this point he was getting frustrated. How hard can it be to find an air filter? He asked a third person, and they said, "In aisle eleven, down on the end, left side." (This was back in the day when items would almost always be in stock.) He went to the location again without success, and in annoyance, he stormed out of the store. My mom was wondering what had happened. It had been at least twenty minutes since he left. They shop there all the time.

Once he returned to the car, they left and headed home. They only lived around the corner. My mom had groceries in the car to bring in and put away, and my brother helped her. He entered the house first. As he did so, he said he sensed something was wrong and had a weird feeling. When he went to set the groceries in the kitchen, he saw the kitchen window was broken. He quickly headed out, and as he went, he looked down the hallway and saw my mom's dresser tipped upside down! They had been robbed, and cops later said it looked like the burglars knew what they were doing. Had my brother and my mom not been delayed at the store, they could have walked in on the robbery and maybe been killed. When things get delayed, God could be protecting us!

Another very difficult experience was when my mom found out she had one of the worst forms of leukemia, namely acute myeloid leukemia. She was a strong believer in God, with a deep faith in Him. She said that one night while lying in bed, she heard God say, "Trust me." Then her brother stopped by with a book for her called *Jesus Calling: Enjoying Peace in His Presence* by Sarah Young. I've never seen the two words "trust me" mentioned more than in that small book. It's a daily devotional that is written as if Jesus is speaking to you each day. I'm so thankful she had the book to carry her through her illness. That book has helped me and my family so much. As I read the words "trust me," I can't help but be amazed at how those were the exact ones she needed to hear at that time. It was put in her path at a perfect time. She had a strong faith that she could be healed, but she was also stoic and realized not everyone gets a healing. And she prayed for God's will to be done, which is the best way to pray. It's not always easy to accept because we want our prayers to go our way. She knew this wasn't Heaven, and this life on Earth isn't perfect. I am so thankful she was spared the worst symptoms.

She had her tough times, but she really wasn't in pain constantly, and she wanted to have her mind stay sharp up until the end, and she did.

Her big hope was for my father to come around and have a relationship with Jesus. My brother has always lived with my parents, and he has always been very protective of my mother. He said my mom was always there for him through all of his surgeries and that he would be there for her. We told them we'd care for our mom, but my brother and dad insisted they would do it. He was the best, most loving son and caregiver I've ever witnessed. Little did we know he was suffering a large, painful growth near his lower spine. He has always been a bleeder, so this was extra dangerous for him. It was a huge blood clot growing in his nerve endings. The doctor told him he had bone cancer.

I was just sick at the news, and now, of all times, I didn't want my mom to know about his diagnosis. But he didn't keep anything from her; they had a special bond. He told her if he had to crawl into her room, he would, just so he could continue to care for her. He did care for her up until the end. She wanted to endure until Mother's Day. I just knew she would pass on Mother's Day, and I thought, *No, Lord, I don't wanna think of her passing on Mother's Day of all days*. But it felt as though God said, "Today she will spend Mother's Day in the arms of her mother." I instantly felt a peace at those words. *I'll see her again*, I thought, *but today she needed to be with her mama*.

We were worried about my brother being so close to my mom; she was his world. But God is faithful, and my brother was covered in a peace that surpasses all understanding. That peace God promises us is priceless!

My brother, the doctors eventually said, did not have bone cancer! They couldn't find any! But he needed to have the surgery, and the doctors were dreading it. They were concerned about getting out the massive blood clot that was growing quickly and wrapped around his nerve endings near the spine. They were concerned about whether he'd ever walk again.

My brother told me the night before the surgery that he begged God to take him home. He had suffered enough on this earth. He laid his clothes out on the bed, fully expecting those to be his burial clothes. He told my dad where to find them. He said that if he couldn't walk, he didn't want to be a burden, and he would rather God take him home to Heaven. Also, the doctor who did his previous surgery when no other doctor would, was involved in this surgery. It took several surgeons to get all of that mass safely removed. It gave us a sense of peace knowing that he was in the hands of the surgeon who'd worked on his spine before and who was familiar with his condition. Needless to say, my brother made it through beautifully, and he can walk! The surgeon said the procedure was extremely difficult and the blood clot mass was the size of a loaf of bread, all wrapped in spinal nerves. It was an absolute miracle he made it through and that he can walk normally!

When he woke up after the surgery, my brother said he was shocked and a little disappointed, as he was ready to be in Heaven. But I told him he was needed here! When it's not our time to go, we can make it through extreme conditions. That's one thing I've realized. I always wonder why you hear the phrase "The good die young." For example, I had one of my best friends die in a car accident in college. She fell asleep at the wheel while driving. She didn't have her seatbelt on and got thrown out through the window. Her boyfriend didn't get a scratch. But then I realized she was ready to be in heaven. Her heart was full of love for Jesus. I feel that's why a lot of criminals or drunks survive: it's because many of them are not believers, and they aren't ready to go. God doesn't want to lose any of His children before they have their hearts ready for Him. He wants to give them every chance He can before He comes back.

Getting back to my brother, I believe he was spared because he was needed. He was a great help and support to my dad. They grew to have a great relationship with one another. It would've been too much for my dad to lose my brother too. My mom got her wish. Through all this, my dad opened his heart to God and developed a close relationship with Jesus. Again, God won't give us more than we can handle, but we do get close!

One thing that was important to my dad was a sign he received. He told my mom to visit him after death if she could. Well, just before she passed, my dad said he saw my mom looking up and waving her hands in the air as if she saw something. And then one day, after she passed, Dad said he saw the back of my mom in one of her dresses in their bedroom. It was just an outline of her image, but he knew it was her. He got his wish. God cares no matter how large or small our desire might be!

A shocking experience I had was after we had Mom's funeral. We came home later that evening, and my husband hung a picture he had printed of my mom in our bedroom. I was on the phone talking to my sister about the picture, and my husband yelled for me to come into the bedroom. He said, "The picture just popped off the wall like someone hit it off. It didn't just drop; it popped up and then down."

I'm glad he witnessed it because if I had, he'd think I exaggerated how it happened. I could tell he was freaked out about it, so I kept saying, "What was that? What was that? What would do that?"

I walked out to get a drink in the kitchen, and the house was dark inside. Then, down the hall, I heard a man's voice say, "It was an angel." He continued to say something else, but I freaked out. That experience scared me almost to death. To be honest, I think I said, "Get the hell out of here. I'm not into that shit!" We never know how we'll react in fear when we find ourselves in a weird situation like that.

I feel bad about my reaction. I'd never had anything like that happen before. With my reaction, I think I scared that angel away. We all react to things differently. I regret not hearing the rest of his message. I've never heard another word again. I share these stories to confirm there is a God. Jesus is real, and He doesn't want any of us to miss going to Heaven when He comes back for us.

PART EIGHT

A few more experiences that have impacted my faith in God follow.

Once I cared for a certain elderly couple who had been married for about seventy years. They were both atheists. Then one night I was up late, and the husband came out to the living room where I was, and he seemed frantic. He said that he'd had a bad dream and that he wanted to hear about the God I talked about. But he said it was too late to start believing because he was ninety years old. I said, "It's never too late. If you are right, and there is nothing after this life, you lose nothing. But if I am right, you lose everything."

A relevant example in the Bible is when Jesus was nailed on the cross. He had a thief on each side of him, and one of them acknowledged that Jesus was the Son of God. Jesus said, "I'll see you up there." (The Gospel of Luke.) So, you see, religion wants to make it complicated, but it is simple. Acknowledge Jesus as the Son of God. Believe and ask for forgiveness. It's that simple. But believe it in your heart.

The next morning that elderly man asked me to pray with him. He wanted to accept Jesus in his heart. After we prayed for him to accept Jesus as the Son of God, he said, "I feel like a kid again." He looked over at his wife and said, "Work on her."

I said, "I will." And he shook his head like he didn't believe she would come around to believing in God. He was sitting in a chair, and he put his head back and closed his eyes. He died five minutes later. That was a shocking moment. Talk about making it just in time. So never think it's too late, but don't put it off either because it could be.

Back to his wife. I thought she had always been an atheist, but I came to learn she used to be a strong believer. When she was young, her sister, who had children, got cancer. So the woman prayed and told everyone God would heal her sister. She said, "God wouldn't leave her children without a mother." Well, this mother ended up dying, and this woman built the thickest wall I've ever seen against God. She became very bitter.

We have to remember this isn't Heaven. We don't understand why, but not everyone is healed. One thing that has helped me as a believer is knowing that if our loved ones who have passed were believers, we will see them again. They aren't our past; they are our future. Remember, if our loved one has passed, hopefully they had asked God to be in their heart before it was too late. Remember, God doesn't want to lose any of us. Hopefully, they had a final chance to choose Him just before passing, a chance that we might not know about.

The man's wife, who was bitter, had more chances to get it right and choose God than I've ever seen. She had about ten chances, getting close to death and coming back from the edge each time. She was stubborn, and God wanted her to come back to Him before she died.

Another experience I had was caring for a wonderful Jewish man. He said, "I don't believe in Jesus."

I asked him, "Why do you believe in the Old Testament and not believe in the New Testament? The Old Testament is the first half of the Bible, and the New Testament is the second half. If you believe in one part of it, why not believe in all of it?"

Well, one day he needed CPR, and my husband helped bring him back from the edge. The first thing he said to me was, "I saw a bright light, and I saw Jesus. And Jesus said, 'Go back!'" Wow, that was amazing for me to hear. Imagine! A nonbeliever saying he saw Jesus!

I remember I once had an elderly woman move into our house, who came from an abusive home and had not been fed well at all. I remember that on her first night with us, I made her favorite meal of fried chicken with mashed potatoes. She was so happy to be out of that other house and was so looking forward to eating her favorite meal. I'll never forget sitting next to her, watching her devour her meal with such joy. It was the first time I'd seen someone eat and enjoy food as if it were their last meal.

When she was done eating, I felt I wanted to pray for her, thankful she was so happy. When I finished the prayer, I looked at her with her head down, and I thought, *Oh no, she looks like she just died.* It literally was her last meal, and I feel she died with a happy heart. Yes, she did die—peacefully. But I couldn't believe it. I couldn't believe I'd have to tell her family that she loved her meal, then we prayed, and she died. I guess if you have to go, then that's a quick, painless way to have it happen. I told my husband, and he said, "Just don't say any prayers for me!"

PART NINE

A difficult time for my husband and I as parents was when all three of our adult children were in separate locations in the country yet all found themselves in dangerous weather. My son was in the Navy on a ship somewhere in the Atlantic Ocean, in the middle of a hurricane. One of my daughters was on a work trip, caught up in Philadelphia in a high-rise building that was swaying in the hurricane winds, and my other daughter was on her honeymoon, leaving Hawaii during an active alert—a tsunami warning. What an unbelievable experience to have all three kids in the middle of natural disasters in different parts of the country on the same day! You learn to be a prayer warrior really quick under such circumstances! God protected all of them! I just don't know how people without faith in God survive in this world.

My daughter Sarah has had a couple of amazing things happen that mean a lot to her.

She and her husband both went to college and have a great deal of student loan debt. When they were looking for their first house, she was discouraged by how much they actually qualified for when it came to securing a home loan. She's a nurse, and he's a pharmacist. She said, "It doesn't seem fair. We worked hard and went to school to have it easier financially, and friends who didn't go to school are qualifying for larger loans." The school debt hurt their income and caused them to qualify for a smaller amount.

Well, she had seen many homes at that stage, and when she saw this one particular house, she fell in love with it! It was her dream home! They put in an offer. Then someone put in a larger cash offer. How can you compete with that? Then her realtor had a glitch in his email system, and he said the only email he received that day was the one to let him know the cash offer fell through. My daughter shouldn't even have gotten this information from the realtor, seeing as his email system was down. This house was a total miracle because it was a quick sale due to divorce, and my daughter and her husband got to see it before it went on the market. Other houses they saw involved people having bidding wars over them. So, this house would've been out of their reach had it gone on the market.

God is so good! I am still amazed that the only email the realtor received was that one! They could've missed out on their dream home. But God had handpicked it for them. Now it's their home they share with four beautiful children. That in itself is a miracle because my daughter had a severe case of uterine fibroids. My gynecologist said it's almost impossible to get pregnant and carry babies to full term with her condition being as bad as it was. She had four difficult pregnancies, but their children are all here, safe and healthy, and they were all full-term pregnancies.

Another miracle in Sarah's path was when she needed

milk for her third baby, as she nursed all her children up to a year. She is a lactation consultant for mothers of newborns and helps educate them on how to breastfeed successfully. There are a lot of techniques to help mothers to breastfeed their babies. It is God's natural way, and if you can manage to breastfeed, it's so much more nutritious for the baby. Well, for one of her children, she just wasn't producing enough milk to feed her, and it was breaking my daughter's heart because she knew how important breast milk was for the baby's development and well-being.

Only God knows how strong a desire is in our hearts. He cares about all of it! So, anyways, in God's perfect timing, someone called her department at work saying his wife is producing a ton of extra milk that their child doesn't need, and they'd like to help some mom in need. They had, like, a freezer full. The couple were both child therapists and were extremely careful and educated about eating well and adding expensive supplements to make the wife's milk as rich as possible. So, the mom was the perfect person to offer this opportunity to another woman. Naturally, my daughter was nervous and a little afraid to use someone else's milk for her baby. But she prayed and couldn't believe the perfect timing, so she decided to take up the generous offer because the couple sounded so kind and thoughtful.

When she went to pick up the milk, she was shocked to discover it was a couple she had worked with. She had helped the mother to be able to nurse her baby as she'd had some difficulty at first! They hit it off beautifully, and my daughter really liked them. Little did my daughter know that she was teaching someone how to nurse successfully who would soon be helping to feed my daughter's own baby in her time of need. Talk about coming around in a full circle. What are the odds of that? God works mysteriously in our favor!

PART TEN

Another meaningful thing happened to me a few years ago when I went on a dream trip to Europe with my daughters. But it was a difficult time because an old injury to my knees was at its worst. The doctor said it was one of the worst bone-on-bone knee conditions he'd ever seen. Well, I've worked on my legs for long hours seven days a week for many years. But I wasn't going to let that stop me from going to visit Europe with my girls. I've always wanted to go back with my kids. I hadn't been back since my last trip there thirty years ago. Well, my two daughters and my two granddaughters were able to go with me, but my son already had a trip planned with his girlfriend. I came to find out we were all at the airport in Brussels at the same time, quite unexpectedly.

The girls and I had missed our connecting flight, so we had an hour's layover in Brussels. I remember thinking, *I wonder where Ryan is?* Little did I know he and his girlfriend were somewhere at the airport, too. Our phone had no reception at the time, so we couldn't call them. But it was ironic to me because I felt bad Ryan wasn't with us on the trip. I'd always wanted to return and show all my kids the Europe I'd fallen in love with. And now, God had us all together. I just didn't know it! The old enemy, the Devil, likes to mess with plans sometimes—like maybe not letting my phone work! But I don't want to give him any credit. God did bless my desire, and all my kids were in Brussels together with me in Europe. The timing of that was truly a miracle.

God was so faithful that He let me climb a mountain in Spain. He helped me climb rocky, steep hills in Greece. I never fell or got hurt despite my knees. I saw other people stumble and fall. I prayed for them. I'm so thankful I got to enjoy that journey without any injuries.

But when I came back home, I realized I needed to get my knees replaced. I've always hated the thought of surgery. I'd never had surgery before, and I was avoiding it like the plague. But enough was enough. I got both knees done within two months of each other. The first knee was easy. The second knee was harder. I'm so glad God takes care of the details so I experienced the less painful leg first, because if it were the other way around, I might not have wanted to get the second knee done. I'm also so thankful God put me in the path of the best surgeon. Plus, the hospital was more like a resort. We could order free, unlimited Starbucks, and the food was prepared by a chef. I love how God cares about the details of our hearts no matter how small or large the details are.

Now I'll be sharing more recent stories, starting with the year 2020. I don't think any of us will forget that year when the world stopped and life-as-usual ended.

My dad woke up one morning, and my brother, who lives with him, found him in the bathroom saying he had trouble breathing and asking him to call 911.

That's not like my dad at all, as he doesn't like to ask for help. Also, Covid was rampant in all the hospitals, and that was the last place he'd want to be, so we knew it was serious. He was admitted to the hospital. His lung had collapsed. He had COPD (chronic obstructive pulmonary disease), with some emphysema. No family members were allowed to see him. He needed surgery to reinflate the lung, and the doctors needed to remove some of the bad lung. At the hospital, he was shocked when the staff came to tell him they had no surgeon available. He wanted to go to the Mayo Clinic thirty miles away, but this would mean another ambulance ride and a wait at another emergency room. It was a scary thought, with all the extra exposure to people sick with Covid in the hospital and him being so weak with his lung condition. For him, it was a very fragile position to be in. He barely made it there alive, but miraculously, he did make it.

Dad survived surgery and never contracted Covid either. It was difficult not to be able to visit him through all of his trauma. Though he ended up getting MRSA (methicillin-resistant *Staphylococcus aureus*), a type of staph bacteria that is resistant to several commonly used antibiotics. It's a true miracle he survived all of that at eighty years of age. Again, I've learned if it's your time, you will go, and if not, you will survive.

Through all of this, I was the only one working in our care home. My husband is a semi-truck driver for my son's company, and he drove all over the country, so he couldn't come home and risk exposing the elderly in our care home to Covid. He would stay in a hotel during this difficult time. He did catch Covid, and he found out when he put on cologne and realized he couldn't smell it. My husband never regained his sense of smell. He self-quarantined in the hotel room. My daughter Sarah, who is a nurse as mentioned, caught Covid from a patient, and she gave it to my other daughter, Ashley, who lived with her. They both became so very sick. She knew they would've gotten hospitalized if they had gone to see a doctor. Sarah has four small children, and the oldest, at seven, took care of everyone—plus some puppies. My son-in-law is a pharmacist, as mentioned, and he had to work many long, stressful hours helping people who had Covid. He never caught it that first year, which is amazing since he was exposed daily, helping those in need. With all his exposure, though, he only got Covid once. God is good and faithful. God will not give us more than we can handle. We were all very close to the limit, though.

I felt helpless at the care home. I was there alone with the three elderly residents for about a year. I felt so helpless with my kids and husband sick. I would make them food when I could, and my son-in-law would pick it up outside our house's front door. I even made protein meatballs for their nursing dog to keep her and her pups strong and healthy. It was such a lonely time. I saw my life passing before me. I had worked thirty-five years helping others, and I just had a strong urge to be with my family. It was such an unbelievable time to be in the most fragile of businesses. None of my elderly residents got Covid, thank God. I was very careful but also very afraid to take in anyone new as a resident or as staff. Our whole business and livelihood could have been gone in a blink.

I talked with the Lord and said, "Lord, I'm ready to

sell and retire and rest and enjoy my family." I thought, *Is there anybody who would be buying this type of business at this time?* I thought nobody would want to touch it with Covid and all the uncertainties going on in the world. I read online how to "sell by owner," also known as "for sale by owner" (FSBO). It refers to a real estate transaction where the property owner sells their property directly to a buyer without the involvement of a real estate agent. I got the property all ready for showing and, hopefully, a sale. Then I noticed the floor in the family room had a piece of flooring come up. It was under warranty, so I called the supplier, and they said they couldn't fix it because it was caused by a water leak and they were not liable for that. It ended up being a huge mess because I needed a whole new sewer line installed! I couldn't believe it! It seemed to be one setback after another.

But I stayed strong, having faith that God cared and knew the desire of my heart. This life isn't always easy. People came to see the house, and several liked it, but they wanted it full, as we were licensed for ten people. They also wanted me to train them for three months before they took over the business. Honestly, that sounded and felt like an eternity. I thought, *Lord, the only one who is going to want this place is someone who already has a care home and can appreciate its potential.* I was throwing everything in the sale, all furniture and appliances, so it would be walk-in ready. Finally, a nurse and a doctor came to see me. They already had several homes and wanted ours instantly, with no training required. What a miracle that in those conditions, namely Covid, God sent the one and only suitable buyer. I got to hand over the keys on my daughter's birthday.

My husband and I moved in with my daughter, son-in-law, and four grandkids. It was an adjustment after being quarantined alone for the year, but it was an amazing blessing to finally be together! God is good!

PART ELEVEN

It was now 2023, and my dad had overcome his obstacles and was doing quite well. My brother insisted he'd take care of my dad, and he did a great job. We offered to help, but he wanted to do it. Well, my dad started to feel ill and was having a lot of blood tests done. He did not tell us much about the results.

My dad's birthday was coming up, and I've always wanted to get him and my brother a large flatscreen TV, but they were stubborn and old-school. They said they didn't need it, but theirs broke, and I thought, *Here's a perfect opportunity to get them a new TV as a birthday present. They can't refuse a gift.*

Earlier, just before my dad's birthday, my husband surprised me, saying he wanted us to take an eleven-day cruise around the time of Dad's birthday. My dad loved travel, like I do, and he insisted we take our cruise, but he looked different to me, and I was concerned.

So, my husband and I surprised my dad with a visit, and we brought the TV plus a sound bar to help my dad's hearing. I brought him some chocolate cake as well, we sang him an early Happy Birthday.

Dad had a doctor's appointment the next day, and I thought if anything was wrong, they'd get him checked out and help him get better. We were also leaving on our cruise the next day. My dad was so happy my husband and I would get to spend some time together on this trip.

I'll never forget the look on Dad's face when he saw the size of the TV we bought as his gift and how good the sound was. He was thrilled. I'm so thankful I made that homemade chocolate cake for him and that I got to sing him an early Happy Birthday. He devoured the cake. Then I asked if he needed any groceries, and he said, "Some milk." But after a minute or two, he told me that what he really needed was a pair of slippers because he was afraid that at the doctor's appointment nothing would fit on his feet because they were swollen. His feet had never been swollen before. I was very concerned but figured the doctor would address any issue and take care of it.

Once I was at the store to buy the milk, my husband called and said that he'd found Dad's list and there were many, many more items he needed. I couldn't believe it, but I took my time to find everything he wanted. He loved to cook, and he had found a few special recipes he was looking forward to making. Just as I finished shopping, I remembered the slippers. They can be difficult to find if it isn't holiday time. But when I looked, I found two comfortable pairs in the size he needed. I thought, *Thank you, Lord. You care more than anyone!*

Oh, I almost forgot to mention I made a stop at Home Depot right at closing time. I just got in the door. I was looking around trying to find a wood plank to balance the TV on because the TV stand at Dad's house was too small. I didn't want the TV to fall, so I thought that would be a temporary solution until we got back from our trip. I didn't expect the worker to be willing to cut the perfect size I needed at closing time, but he was so kind he insisted on helping me. I just looked up, thinking, *Thank you, Lord, for putting the right person in my path and getting me in that store by seconds before they closed!* So, about two and a half hours later, I made it back to the house.

My husband said he had the best talk ever with my dad that night. My dad was so appreciative. I'll never forget the look on my dad's face when he saw the slippers. The first pair was way too small with his swelling. But the second pair fit him perfectly. They were warm and comfortable, with a non-skid bottom. I looked in his eyes, and I saw pure joy and relief. You would think I gave him a piece of gold. The satisfaction of helping someone in need is priceless. Just taking the time to be kind and helpful is worth far more than receiving any gift yourself. I learned that from helping and caring for elderly people all those years.

That's why I want to encourage anyone reading this to go out and do something kind for others. It doesn't matter how big or small the task is; kindness is free. If you have the means or money to do bigger things, do it. The feeling and reward you will receive from doing it will far outweigh the feeling you get from buying yourself something. It's a great way to feel better about life by getting your mind off yourself and your problems. Whoever you come into contact with, make it a habit of doing something kind. It is healing and better than any medicine!

It breaks my heart to say, but that was the last time I saw my dad alive. He fell while getting out of the car after the doctor's appointment, and everything snowballed after that.

PART TWELVE

I want to share some details about how, during this most difficult situation, God was faithful and covered me in the peace I mentioned earlier.

First of all, we were on our cruise in the middle of the ocean. We had phone service, but it didn't work all the time; often there was no reception. It was very frustrating, but somehow, while on our cruise, we received four calls. I still can't get over how the four most important calls came through when we should not have received any of them. The first call was from my daughter to tell me my dad had taken a turn for the worst but could still pull through. Then my son called and said Grandpa was craving a beer. So my son took it up to the hospital, and my dad enjoyed it enormously. I got to talk to my dad, and he said he was so happy we got to go on our trip. I got to tell him I love him. My son said he had the best visit with his grandpa. All the cousins got to spend some time with Grandpa as well. I'm so thankful for those little moments God allowed them to have together. Then I got the call from my daughter to say they did everything they could to save Dad, but he was bleeding out. He still had clarity of mind, and even though he had a close relationship with Jesus, he was scared to die.

It was a weird feeling to know Dad knew he was dying, and he wanted to live. But he knew the medical team had said there was nothing more they could do. They explained that his body would shut down, and his heart would stop, probably within twenty-four to forty-eight hours. I can't imagine what he was feeling. It almost felt like an assisted suicide, for lack of a better word. But the amazing thing is I got to talk to my dad and pray with him. I got to tell him about something my mom taught me to do, which had helped me while I was healing from my knee surgeries. Before you get out of bed, she'd told me, squeeze your right hand and look up to Jesus, and say, "I am blood of your blood, bone of your bone, and flesh of your flesh." There is power in those words. Also, when you squeeze your right hand and look up, it's like saying, "Jesus, you have my hand, and you are with me every step of the way." Then you know you are never alone! I told Dad I'd take him with me on all my journeys because I got my travel bug from him.

The last call was from my son to tell me Dad had passed. I was sitting on the deck at the stern of the ship, looking at the most beautiful turquoise waters in Aruba. As hard as it was, God covered me in peace. It's hard to explain, but I was so thankful for it. I forgot to mention that during the first call from my daughter, she said, "Mom, I'm so glad you aren't here because it would break your heart to see what is going on with your brother and sister." My children said it would've killed me or put me in the hospital to witness it. I'll never understand it. I can't believe this is part of my story. I hate to have to share it, but I want to be honest so you know how faithful God was through one of the most shocking things to happen in my life. I know there are many people out there who are hurting. People who've had awful, horrible things happen to them where family, friends, spouses, or leaders of their church have wounded and betrayed them.

When I came home from my cruise, we had my father's funeral, and it was awkward and very uncomfortable seeing my brother and sister after my kids told me how they were acting.

I've heard how families can change when a loved one dies. I've seen it in the families I've cared for, but I never would've dreamed it could happen to my family. We were all Christian believers, and I thought I had a close relationship with my brother and sister. The day after the funeral, I met with my brother and sister at my dad's house. It turned out my sister was the executor of my dad's trust even though I was the oldest sibling. I knew this because on one of my recent visits, while my dad had some tests done at the hospital, he told me, "I trust you as much as your brother and sister, but I don't trust your husband because of what happened in the past."

So, while at the house, the first thing my brother said was, "It's mine. Everything is mine." We all agreed my dad should leave a good amount to cover my brother's medical issues, but he also had his own good healthcare insurance. My sister said the trust was only for her and my brother, and the details of my dad's trust document were for their eyes only. She made me feel like my dad didn't want me to know anything about it. I didn't believe that. She also said she'll only tell me what she wants me to know. It seemed like a control issue. I asked her if I could see a copy of his trust document and wishes. She and my brother refused. They were both so mean to me. I couldn't believe they were the same people. If I had not witnessed their behavior, I wouldn't have believed it. Finally, she left to get a copy of the trust. I read it out loud. I didn't see anything that said only they could see it. I just wanted to know my dad's last wishes. It also mentioned a will. I asked them if there was a will, and they both shouted, "No!" But my dad was organized and detailed, and I knew he would have a will. When I read the trust document, I saw the name of the lawyer who was involved, and I remembered it.

It was heartbreaking to see how my siblings were acting. Well, I finally got in touch with the lawyer and said I'd like to pick up a copy of the trust to look it over. When I did, enclosed was a copy of my dad's will, and it said a copy was kept at the house. So, I now knew they'd seen it and were just lying. After I read it, it said that the proceeds of the sale of all personal items were to be distributed to all his kids equally. It's not like he had a lot, but it was a considerable amount. I learned my brother and sister were not who I thought they were. It seemed everything coming out of their mouths were lies.

It's unbelievable how money, power, control, and greed can change a person. It's probably one of the ugliest things I've ever witnessed. I see how it destroys families. So, I felt I'd not only lost my dad but my brother and sister too. I was upset at them and hurt. I still prayed for them, but I was no longer in a relationship with them. We can't pick who our family is, but we can pray for them. God says to pray for our enemies. If family members are toxic to be around, I don't think you have to surround yourself with them. Through this difficult time, the only constant in all of it was God being with me, protecting me, and covering me in peace so I could get through it. I've chosen to stay thankful for the last day with my dad. I'm thankful for getting the important calls that should not have come through given the circumstances at sea. I'm thankful I got to pray with my dad and tell him I love him. I'm choosing to dwell on the good moments. Just squeeze your right hand and look up! He will get you through anything!

PART THIRTEEN

I want to add a very important detail I learned during this awful situation after my dad's passing. My son asked me why I don't become angrier with my brother and sister and fight them on this. Through most of this experience, I stayed pretty calm only because God covered me in peace. I remember feeling like I was part of a story in Genesis in the Bible's Old Testament, the one about two brothers, Jacob and Esau, and their father, Isaac, who was old and blind. Isaac wanted to give his oldest son, Esau, his blessing and birthright, and the younger brother, Jacob, went to his father wearing a disguise, trying to steal this from his brother. My siblings made me feel they were stealing the portion my father wanted me to have.

But I've always heard that God says, "Move out of the way and pray for your enemies, and I will fight your battle for you." He will vindicate us. We don't have to fight; He will make the wrongs right. So that is what I told my son I'm trying to do—to watch God take control. All I can say is it was amazing to watch how God addressed that situation. All Dad's children and anyone named in the trust document could attend the lawyer's meeting. It turned out my father thought carefully about how he could look out for all family members fairly, and he did think of all of us. The shocker was my sister and brother getting reprimanded by the lawyer and told that they'd better watch everything they do, because he knew we'd all keep them accountable. I just wanted to make sure everyone received their fair share, as my father wished for his estate to be handled.

Then the bombshell dropped that my dad had left some money for each great-grandchild who'd already been born, but it stopped there. My sister's and her husband's jaws dropped because they had no grandchildren yet, and no future grandchildren could benefit directly from my dad's trust and will. They were like, "You mean none of our future grandkids get anything?" The lawyer said no and that it would be a big deal to change Dad's wishes because everyone involved would need to sign a new agreement. Well, after how they had treated everyone, several refused to sign it. I did feel bad for them when I heard that, but you reap what you sow, and the way you treat people can come back to bite you. I have never seen stronger vindication in my life, and I didn't have to say a word. It felt as though a higher power was correcting them for their actions.

Also, I need to share how, most recently, God worked through my other sister, who had been estranged from the family for many, many years. She always felt left out and considered herself the black sheep of the family. Ironically, she was the only one I was able to connect with after my dad passed. Well, I made peace with her, and she was getting ready to move to Florida in a couple of days, and we said our goodbyes. But then she sent me a text asking me if she could ask a big favor of me. She asked me to reach out and make peace with my other sister and my brother.

I told her I needed time to talk with God about it. I was surprised how long it took me to release this feeling about them. I just had no desire to have a relationship with my other sister and my brother. I felt anything coming out of their mouths would be lies anyway. I honestly wished them well and would pray for them, so I thought that was good enough. But my sister said a few things that hit me and opened my eyes, as if I were just hearing it for the first time. God often does that—He'll put a person in our path and have them maybe say the same thing we've heard many times before. But when it's the perfect timing, it'll be as if our eyes have the blinders off or we are hearing these same words for the first time.

So I asked my sister to call them and set the meeting up at her house that very night. I gave my brother and my other sister each a hug, and I said I forgave them and asked them to forgive me if I'd ever said anything to hurt them. We talked a little, and then I said how ironic it was that God worked through the most unlikely person in the family to bring us together for a healing. And just before she moved to Florida! I am thankful I met with them. I have peace in my heart now. I've handed it all to God, and I've moved on. I continue to pray for them. I text them once in a while or share prayer requests.

I thought if I'm asking you guys to find forgiveness regarding others and your past, I have to be willing to do the same. I'm so glad I did because my heart and spirit have a much lighter feeling! I pray you find the strength and courage to do the same. Just lay it down and remove the weight from your neck and shoulders caused by any hurt or wrong someone has done to you. You don't deserve to carry that weight around. Set yourself free of it. It's up to them what they decide to do with their guilt, but you deserve to be set free of the pain of it all. You are well worth it!

PART FOURTEEN

I'm sharing this most recent discovery that popped up on YouTube one day while I was searching the internet. It was as though God revealed answers and truth to help me understand a few very difficult people in my life. It was like a light switch had been turned on, and I recognized who I'd been dealing with—narcissists. This information helped answer many of the questions I'd had concerning their bizarre behavior and has taught me how to deal with them. Communicating with such people prior to this knowledge was miserable and a mystery. All communication left me exhausted and without answers. It was all confusion and conflict, with no closure. But with this new information, I have found the peace and understanding that I've been seeking for many years.

I want to share the name of this helpful counselor I found on YouTube. Her name is Kris Reece. She specializes in dealing with narcissists, whom she calls "toxic people." These are people with particular traits that make them very difficult to deal with. If you have to interact with someone in your life who is relentless in being self-obsessed, self-serving, unfair, and difficult, and who seems to enjoy hurting you emotionally, then I urge you to look her up.

Kris Reece says a great way to deal with a narcissist is to start every morning practicing putting on the armor of God. Mentally envision putting on each piece of protection over your body. (It says this in the Bible too, Ephesians 6:10–18.) For example, put on your shoes of peace. Put on the belt of truth. Put on your armor to cover your heart and your back so no hurtful arrows penetrate you. Put on your helmet to protect your mind from bad, destructive thoughts. Hold up your shield in your right hand and your sword in your left hand, representing the word of God.

You don't have to respond to any of the venom directed at you by the narcissist because you know you have God's protection. Don't let any of their deceitful words penetrate your being. You will feel God's peace and protection. It will bother them if you don't show any emotion or reaction to what they're saying or doing. Showing no reaction, only the calm you feel, will drive them crazy. Don't engage with them or offer any response. Just stand there confidently and calmly and look them in the eye, knowing the truth and that God is protecting you. You don't want to engage and add any fuel to the fire. That way, there will be no fighting or energy wasted because there is no way to change how they think, other than God performing a miracle. They can fight with themself. You don't have to be dragged into the mud with them. You may want to just calmly say, "If that's what you feel, fine," and just quietly walk away and be busy doing something else.

Finding Kris Reece on YouTube was due to God's perfect timing because I had never heard of her or heard anything about narcissistic behavior before, and I was busy finishing this letter to you. When her YouTube video popped up, I took the time to check it out, and it was an answer to a lot of unanswered questions I've had for many years. I wish I'd found her sooner, but God's timing is perfect, and I found it just in time to share it with you guys! I pray it helps you as much as it has me. I know it's a very difficult situation to deal with, but with her guidance and God's strength, it will help to make dealing with such people more bearable.

Kris Reece gives advice on what to do in each situation when dealing with toxic people. I want to add that I'm very new to learning how to deal with narcissistic behavior, so I recommend that if this sort of behavior sounds familiar, like that of someone you're dealing with, then look her up. She has opened my eyes to their common behavior and how to cope with it. I also found the name of Jordon Peterson on YouTube. He is a Canadian Psychologist and author. He has insightful wisdom in saying how a narcissist affects a woman. He was spot on. All I can say is that even just getting answers has helped me understand them better. And it has given me a peace in understanding who I'm dealing with, why nothing has changed, and why nothing will most likely ever change with them. Like I've said, God will randomly put people in our path when we need them most. Finding them is an example of that promise.

PART FIFTEEN

As I prepare to finish this letter, I feel God urging me to share two more stories. One of the stories I wasn't planning to share because I live with it in my heart with great regret. It's an unfinished story. Now, as I look back, it should've been a major story in my letter. I woke up this morning with a heavy heart because during the early hours, the details of this story replayed in my mind over and over again. I asked God, "Why can't I let this go, Lord? It hurts me to think about it." I kept asking Him why it lies so strongly on my mind and to please relieve me of it. And then it hit me: *Lord, do you want me to share this? I don't know why, but maybe it will help someone else.* All I can say is that when I said, "Okay, Lord, I'll put it in this letter," I felt a burden lift off my shoulders and a peace descend that I've never felt before about this incident.

I'm learning to be quiet, trying to listen to His voice. He will put thoughts in your mind. Listen carefully and pray that the thought is of Him and His will. At times, I feel I am a slow learner. It is a process. I'm finding more quiet time with God, and His voice gets clearer the more you seek Him.

Randomly, the memory of events would just pierce my heart with regret. This story involves my second beautiful daughter, Ashley. This incident happened in 2012 in Phoenix, Arizona, at a Chipotle Mexican Grill at Norterra. I was casually eating lunch with my other beautiful daughter, Sarah, when I happened to look back at the people in line, and I saw this very tall young man. All I could think of was my daughter Ashley! I have never before had such strong thoughts when seeing a person. The young man went and sat down across the room, eating by himself. He had excellent posture and mannerisms. He ate so politely. He had an aura around him that I cannot explain. I felt mesmerized. I know it sounds ridiculous. I've never had this happen before or since.

During this whole time, I had a strong urge to go outside and follow when he left to ask him whether he's available and if he'd be willing to go on a blind date with a special girl. I would also have told him at once that I felt a strong urgency to ask him this and that I trusted it was God's will. I'd ask God to make it so I didn't appear too crazy. This urge was so strong I almost couldn't stay in my seat. It was unbelievable. Unfortunately, I felt paralyzed in my chair. I couldn't get up. I felt insecure, not looking my best. It was one of those times when you go out, but you hope you don't run into anyone you know. I missed my opportunity because I let my self-doubt get in the way. My daughter Ashley was going to church, volunteering at church, and tithing, and I think it was a perfect time, and God wanted to bless her. Little did I know she was praying for someone special to come into her life, and I found out from my other daughter, Sarah, that Ashley's dream guy was tall, at six feet five inches. I could almost guarantee this guy was probably that height.

I strongly feel I missed this opportunity when God put an amazing person in my daughter's path, and I didn't do my part. I didn't listen. I've regretted that every day since. I just wonder, what if? God doesn't force us to make a decision. He gives us the free will to choose. It may sound silly to people, but God works mysteriously, and He cares about the desires of our hearts. I'll never forget it because it felt like He was screaming for me to get up and just trust Him. All the guy could've said was no.

So, she still hasn't found that amazing guy out there, but if it's not the right person, it's better to be alone. So, if this ever happens to someone, pray it's the Lord's will, and I say, follow it through! I so wish I did for my daughter's sake. So now I just pray God's will for her life will unfold in good time. I tell God, "Lord, you are a God of second chances, and if it's your will, give me that experience again, and I won't miss it!"

The other story that just came to mind, and I can't believe I almost forgot to share it, happened many years ago. My son and I had a weekend staycation at a local timeshare where we got an inexpensive offer to stay at the property. It was a beautiful place in Scottsdale. My son and I went on a walk around the grounds and saw a man just standing there enjoying the view. He called us over.

I want to mention that getaways were always important to me because we were so busy at the care home with little opportunity to have a break. To get away and have some private, uninterrupted quality time together meant everything to me. Also, we didn't have the chance to get away very often, and rarely could we all go together as a family. Someone always had to be at the care home.

I somewhat reluctantly walked over to the guy because I really just wanted to enjoy time with my boy on a quiet walk. But I'm so glad I did take the time to talk to that man because I feel it was one of those life-changing moments where God put someone in my path when I needed it most.

You know how I've told you my passion is travel? I love seeing the world God has given us to enjoy. And coming from the adventures in Europe and then going straight into a rewarding but stressful, time-consuming life of seven-days-a-week caregiving was not easy. We mostly always did the work ourselves because it was difficult to find caring, dependable help you could trust with the fragile lives we were responsible for.

So, when this man said, "Can you hear that pop of the bottle going off?" I was curious. He said every time you hear the pop of the champagne bottle opening, it's a new timeshare owner paying over $30,000 for one week a year! I couldn't believe it. He said he had a friend who sold wholesale timeshare condos in South Africa at a low price. The deals were, like, five weeks a year for $1,500 in total. We acquired some of these timeshare packages. They have traded strongly to this day and have blessed my family and others with some amazing trips and memories together. I am so very thankful this man was in our path and shared something that has blessed our lives over and over!

I want to add how I was able to get creative with those timeshare condo packages I bought. I would find vacations for people in a barter club, and I would exchange that for many services, such as food from restaurants, dental services, plumbing, carpeting, tile flooring, pest control, auto repairs, and basically anything you'd pay cash for. It became a savings account for everything we needed. So those condos not only blessed us with priceless vacations but have also blessed us in so many other unimaginable ways.

PART SIXTEEN

Forgive me if I'm repetitive as I close this letter, but I want to recap and remind you of some important details as you go on this new journey. Remember, please don't let the crazy leaders and unfair rules that man makes in the name of religion turn your heart from God. A relationship with Jesus is the only thing that will fill you with peace in this empty world. Simply look up and know it's all between you and Him. It is as easy as asking Him to come into your heart by praying these words: "Lord, I believe you are the one and only God who sent your son to die on the cross and arise from death for me to have a chance at eternal life. I ask you to forgive me my sins. Make me fresh and new. Fill me with the peace you promise."

Just talk to God daily about everything you're feeling, whether it's good or bad. Make Him your best and most trusted friend. Again, I encourage you to read the Holy Bible. Start with the Book of Matthew. The NIV version is easier to understand, as I mentioned. After reading the Book of Matthew, you will have a better understanding of who Jesus was and is, and it will be easy to fall in love with the Son of God. He will fill that empty spot in your heart—He's the only one who can. He's what you've been searching for to fill that emptiness. Remember, Jesus will never stop loving you or leave you. Keep your eyes off man and look up. Keep your eyes and heart on what Jesus represents. You are new and whole in Him. Thank God for every new day, and look around to see all the blessings He puts in your path. See with new eyes! I'll be praying for your healing every day.

Also, I would like to share some things that have helped me get closer to Jesus in my relationship with Him.

I recommend reading the book *Jesus Calling: Enjoying Peace in His Presence* by Sarah Young.

I also enjoy Pastor Joel Osteen's weekly televised services. I love his simple messages. They are full of hope and easy to understand. He is a great encourager in a negative, stressful world.

A woman named Lauren Daigle sings beautiful Christian songs. Please listen to her on YouTube. A couple of her songs that have helped me during difficult times are "Rescue" and "You Say." Please listen to the words; it is as if God is speaking to you through them.

Also, please look up the video *Interview with God* at interviewwithgod.com. It's beautiful. (Note that I am not referring to the movie of the same name.)

Please listen to KLove Radio, a Christian radio station. They play positive and encouraging songs. So often when I turn it on, the perfect song will be playing at the moment I need those words the most. God's good at doing that. The radio producers also challenge you to only listen to that station for thirty days and see how it transforms your life. You'll never listen to music in the same way again.

I would also like to recommend watching the movie *The Shack* and reading the book on which it is based, written by William Paul Young. Watch the movie closely and listen to every word. It helps to explain why God loves all His children and why He doesn't want to lose any of them. The theme of the movie is not easy to watch. In the movie, God appears as a woman. But just remember that He can come and visit us in any form. He's mysterious that way. I thought the movie explained, from God's point of view, how He feels about all of His children.

Please watch a new movie out called "Mully " on Angel Studios. This amazing true story will inspire you how one person has the potential to change the world for the better! Also, this is my favorite verse in the Bible, Isaiah 40:31 (NIV):

… but those who hope in the Lord will renew their strength. They will soar on wings like eagles; they will run and not grow weary, they will walk and not be faint.

Powerful and so true!

Another favorite Bible verse is Jeremiah 29:11 (NIV):

"… For I know the plans I have for you," declares the Lord, "plans to prosper you and not to harm you, plans to give you hope and a future."

Please memorize these two Bible verses and keep them in your heart.

Another favorite of mine is a poem by Kent M Keith, called Paradoxical Commandments. Kent Keith has given me permission to include this.

Paradoxical Commandments
By Kent M Keith

1. People are illogical, unreasonable, and self-centered. Love them anyway.

2. If you do good, people will accuse you of selfish ulterior motives. Do good anyway.

3. If you are successful, you will win false friends and true enemies. Succeed anyway.

4. The good you do today will be forgotten tomorrow. Do good anyway.

5. Honesty and frankness make you vulnerable. Be honest and frank anyway.

6. The biggest men and women with the biggest ideas can be shot down by the smallest men and women with the smallest minds. Think big anyway.

7. People favor underdogs but follow only top dogs. Fight for a few underdogs anyway.

8. What you spend years building may be destroyed overnight. Build anyway.

9. People really need help but may attack you if you do help them. Help people anyway.

10. Give the world the best you have and you'll get kicked in the teeth. Give the world the best you have anyway.

Copyright Kent M Keith 1968, renewed 2001

I recall that when I first wanted to write about my experiences, it felt as though God was putting it in my heart to call this letter *The Power of the Spoken Word.* I have learned how powerful the words we say are. I remember the few words Jesus spoke to me and how powerful they were: "I'm coming very, very soon!" Always be careful and always choose your words wisely. So, speak out what you want to be and bring life to your words. God hears them!

I also want to strongly remind you that God's timing is much different than ours. Twenty years to us could be the blink of an eye for God. An important reminder is that just because we have a close relationship with God, it doesn't mean our lives are going to be easy. This isn't Heaven. We have sin and corruption and evil on this earth. But having God and His peace makes it all worthwhile, and if I've learned anything through this rollercoaster of life, it is that the only constant is God's faithfulness in covering us in peace while we are going through the storms and tough times in life. He never leaves us, and He will stop and put little blessings in our path if we slow down enough to look, listen, and see them. He will get us through the tough times, and we will experience joy again! He's so worth trusting.

God has put it in my heart to challenge all of you. I challenge those of you who are willing to open your hearts and give God a second chance to trust Him and let Him back in your heart. Or maybe, for you, it will be the first time you're choosing to believe in Him and want to start a personal relationship with Him to just set yourself free and to show others in your path how to find what you have found by simply showing kindness to them. Whoever you come in contact with. Simple acts of kindness are free, but showing kindness one person at a time will change this world for the better. We are at a time now more than ever when we need to be kind and accept each other just as we are.

Remember, God wants it to be simple. A personal relationship with Him. Start each day by waking up and talking to Him, thanking Him for always being with you, and asking Him to surprise you with His goodness. Look for ways to help others, and you'll be full of peace and joy. I dare you to give it a try! If everything else has failed, why not?

Again, please write to me if you have given yourself a second or first chance to get back to God and share your story. I'd love to hear from you! Remember, your journey won't be easy, but it will be well worth it! I promise.

Contact me at GodsPeaceHeals@gmail.com.

POSTSCRIPT

Before I end this letter, I want to share that a friend reached out to me one day and asked if I had restored good relationships with my siblings. She and I had a few conversations, and she shared how, after their mother died, she and her siblings lost their relationships with one another under circumstances similar to my own. She said that after nine years, they've finally made peace and got together again. She said her sister had never met her grandchildren!

I don't want to wait nine years, I thought, *especially since my sister now has her first grandchild.* I know I told you I forgave her and that I prayed for her, but I still had no desire to have a relationship with her. I was afraid to open that door and to trust her again. My friend shared the same feelings I had. Even though I did feel lighter in spirit after forgiving my sister, it has taken baby steps to get there. It's a process that takes time, and everyone heals differently.

But I can say that when I thought about it taking my friend and her sister nine years to heal their rift, I instantly felt I wanted to call my sister, and I did. We had the best visit in years. It was a big, healing step for me. What felt good and different was that I actually wanted to talk to her for the first time since all of this business with our dad's trust and will happened.

When I was done talking with my friend, she shared that she found a poem that she sent to her sister after talking with her. It's called "Later"by Boucar Diouf,a famous French Canadian writer and storyteller.

It is so powerful and true that I would love for you to please look it up on the internet and read it.

Thank you for reading my letter.